Exploring Leaves

by Kristin Sterling

first step nonfiction

Lerner Publications Company · Minneapolis

I see **leaves**.

Parts of a Plant

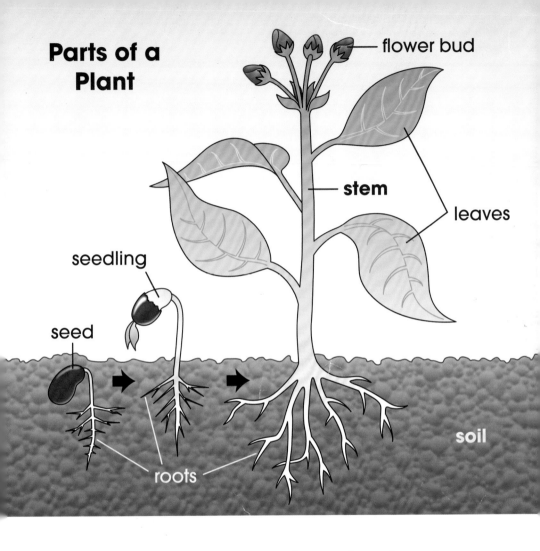

flower bud

stem

leaves

seedling

seed

roots

soil

Leaves are parts of plants.

Each plant part has a job.

Plants need leaves to grow.

Leaves grow on stems.

Stems hold leaves up to the sun.

Stems bring water from the
soil to the leaves.

Leaves use sunlight, water, and air to make food.

Some leaves change colors
in the fall.

Some leaves stay green all
year.

Some plants have small leaves.

Some plants have big
leaves.

Pine trees have leaves like
sharp **needles**.

Gingko plants have leaves shaped like fans.

Leaves are all around you.

Do you see leaves?

All Kinds of Leaves

Leaves with
one blade

Leaves with more
than one blade

Leaves that
change colors

Leaves that
stay green

Big leaves

Small leaves

19

Facts about Leaves

 People need green, leafy plants to live.

 Many families rake leaves in the fall. Kids play in the piles.

 People eat some kinds of leaves, like spinach, lettuce, and cabbage.

 Don't touch a poison ivy plant! The oils can cause an itchy rash and blisters. The rule: leaves of three—let it be!

Koala bears love eating the leaves of the eucalyptus tree!

 A maple leaf is on the flag of Canada.

 Gel from the leaves of aloe vera plants can be used to heal small cuts and burns.

 Mint leaves and basil leaves smell wonderful and can be used in recipes.

Glossary

 leaves – the green parts of a plant that make food

 needles – the long, thin leaves of a pine tree

 soil – the dirt in which plants grow

 stem – the part of a plant that holds up the plant

Index

The images in this book are used with the permission of: © Asia Images/SuperStock, pp. 2, 22 (1st from top); © Laura Westlund/Independent Picture Service, pp. 3, 22 (3rd from top); © Cultura/Alamy, p. 4; © Hannu Viitanen/Dreamstime.com, p. 5; © James Martin/Dreamstime.com, p. 6; © Pangfolio/Dreamstime.com, pp. 7, 22 (bottom); © Andreas Gradin/Dreamstime.com, p. 8; © age fotostock/SuperStock, p. 9; © Jiong Dai/Dreamstime.com, p. 10; © Theo Allofs/CORBIS, p. 11; © Burazin/Iconica/Getty Images, p. 12; © Thanatonauti/Dreamstime.com, p. 13; © Fei Li/Dreamstime.com, pp. 14, 22 (2nd from bottom); © Stone2010/Dreamstime.com, p. 15; © Tim Pannell/CORBIS, p. 16; © LWA/Dann Tardif/Blend Images/Getty Images, p. 17; © National Geographic Image Collection/Alamy, p. 18 (top); © WILDLIFE GmbH/Alamy, p. 18 (center); © Viktor Pravdica/Dreamstime.com, p. 18 (bottom); © Mary Lane/Dreamstime.com, p. 19 (top); © Jelena Selivanova/Dreamstime.com, p. 19 (center); © Bon Appetit/Alamy, p. 19 (bottom).

Front cover: © Liubomir Turcanu/Dreamstime.com

Main body text set in ITC Avant Garde Gothic 21/25. Typeface provided by Adobe Systems.

Lerner Publications Company
A division of Lerner Publishing Group, Inc.
241 First Avenue North
Minneapolis, MN 55401 U.S.A.

Website address: www.lernerbooks.com

Library of Congress Cataloging-in-Publication Data

Sterling, Kristin.
    Exploring leaves / by Kristin Sterling.
        p.   cm. — (First step nonfiction—Let's look at plants)
    Includes index.
    ISBN 978–0–7613–5780–3 (lib. bdg. : alk. paper)
    1. Leaves—Juvenile literature. 2. Plant anatomy—Juvenile literature. I. Title. II. Series: First step nonfiction. Plant parts.
    QK649.S74 2012
    581.4'8—dc22   2010042987

Manufactured in the United States of America
1 – PC – 7/15/11